St. Fidgeta and Other Parodies

ST. FIDGETA

AND OTHER PARODIES

BY

John Bellairs

ILLUSTRATED BY

Marilyn Fitschen

THE MACMILLAN COMPANY : NEW YORK
COLLIER-MACMILLAN LIMITED : LONDON

AUTHOR'S NOTE

I would like to thank my friends, Dale and Marilyn Fitschen, for all their help. They suffered through endless readings from the *Urtext* and gave me many suggestions and ideas. I would also like to thank my friend Bernard Kent Markwell, to whom St. Fidgeta first appeared on a rainy day in front of the Oriental Institute in Chicago. He was struck to the ground by the vision, and after he had rolled about for a bit, he got up and told me what he had seen. He also gave me many ideas: in fact, if you do not like some part of this book, you may attribute it to him.

JOHN BELLAIRS

December, 1965

CONTENTS

St. Fidgeta and Other Parodies

I

THE TRUE HISTORY OF ST. FIDGETA, VIRGIN AND MARTYR

In 482 A.D., St. Fidgeta was born of Christian parents in the little village of Stercoraria in southern Gaul. Like the lives of most people who lived in the fifth century A.D., her little life was rather dull, until her parents were overrun by a foraging band of Avars. Fidgeta was left in the care of her pagan *Left to her* uncle, Leitotes, who sent her to a pagan grammar *pagan uncle* school, where almost every day the sacred mysteries of her religion were held up to ridicule. Her teacher, the notorious skeptic Putricordes, would frequently quote from Porphyry's now lost attack on Christianity. It is through her faithful, if reluctant, note-taking that the only known fragment of this odious work *A hateful book* has been passed down to us. A wax tablet (preserved in the convent of the Fidgettines in Fobbio) bears her name and "JMJ" at the top, and has farther down the page a note, which is labeled "Jocus Porphyris." A rough translation of the corrupt Late Latin would run thus:

Q. Why does a Christian cross himself?

A. To get to the other side.

Scholars agree that the joke seems to lose something in translation.

Despite her diligence, Fidgeta crossed the pagan teacher constantly. During workshop, she would string rosaries or plait penitential whips; throughout the morning idolatry sessions, she would fidget ceaselessly and mumble forbidden prayers. Once she was even caught with an inkwell full of holy water. Finally, during a Sunday morning class in March of 489, she fidgeted so much in her desire to go to Mass that the distraught pedagogue slapped her to death. She was canonized in 490, after she cured Zephyrinus the Anchorite of the nervous shakes.

Facts About St. Fidgeta

St. Fidgeta is the patroness of nervous and unmanageable children. Her shrine is the church of Santa Fidgeta in Tormento, near Fobbio in southern Italy. There one may see the miraculous statue of St. Fidgeta, attributed to the Catholic Casting Company of Chicago, Illinois. This statue has been seen to squirm noticeably on her feast day, and so on that day restless children from all over Europe have been dragged to the shrine by equally nervous, worn-out, and half-mad parents. Though no diminution has

The Fidgettine Convent near Fobbio

been noticed in the fidgeting of those children, the feeling is that the restlessness will at least be converted into meritorious work by the action of the saint. On this point see Tertullian, who proves that fidgeting is (or can be) useful unto salvation. Also,

Fidgeting and mysticism see Gregory of Mopsuestia, on fidgeting as a prelude to mystical experience.

The Fidgettines

Santa Fidgeta in Tormento was built on the spot where St. Fidgeta appeared in 1272 to Scintilla Sforza, who became Mother Latifundia, foundress of the Order of Faithful Fidgettines (O.F.F.). Scintilla, before her vision a spendthrift of checkered reputation, notorious for her midnight levées in the ruins of the Golden House of Nero, was so moved by the miraculous experience that she forsook all earthly joys and wrung from her father, a rich Florentine banker, the eight-hundred acre tract on which

A fortress of chastity she built the first Fidgettine convent. This fortress of chastity crowns a high hill near Fobbio, and today visitors may inspect its eighteen-foot-thick walls, its crenelated towers, and its now empty cannon embrasures. On the hillside below, happy tenant farmers work the vast Fidgettine estate as they have for years, though the sisters have now moved to a new chrome and glass high-rise convent built for them by a Sicilian charitable organization.

St. Adiposa at Work

The order flourished and spread under the guidance of its patroness, and the following saints stud its history like jewels of lambent flame:

St. Pudibunda, who on her wedding night decided that God had called her to a life of spotless virginity. The causes of her death that very night are not known, but the pious may guess at them. She was posthumously admitted to the order.

St. Adiposa, author of numerous anti-ascetic tracts. She decided that a life intentionally cut short by overweight could be consecrated to God. Confined to her cell by immobility much of her life, she *An epic hymn* wrote a long, strangely moving hymn to St. Fidgeta in which the saint is compared to a peach, a plum, a whortleberry, and various other comestibles. The last few stanzas, written in the author's old age, show signs of creative degeneration and are usually omitted.[1] They compare St. Fidgeta to a sugar cone, a bonbon, and, finally, to a squab,

> Browned in the oven of the Father's Light,
> Stuffed with grace and with sage advice.

St. Adiposa died at 93 when the floor of her cell collapsed. Her life principle of caloric immolation

---

[1] Professor Schwiegermutter disagrees in his *Das Fidgetaslied und der Deutsche Geist* (Lüneberg, 1872), 16 vols. He regards these verses as the culmination of Metaphysical imagery.

St. Dragomira at Work

caused much debate about her status as a martyr, but the Council of Trent shelved the matter, and there it stands.

St. Dragomira, the warrior nun of Bosnia. Converted from paganism by the Fidgettine missionary Anfractua, she spent her life in fomenting religious wars and is usually credited with Christianizing Upper Bosnia. She was clubbed to death by her pagan brother Bogeslaw, after a long and heated argument about Christian hate. Patroness of edged weapons.

St. Fidgeta in Art

St. Fidgeta's marks in art are the red slap mark on the cheek, the Scholar's pen, and the virgin's girdle. Early representations of her are rare, since the stasis of Byzantine art does not permit the depiction of a restless saint. There may, however, have been an icon of St. Fidgeta in the monastery of the Studium in Constantinople. On the other hand, there may not have been. But if it did exist, it was probably destroyed when the Emperor Isaac Comnenus smashed the furnishings of the Studium and made his half-brother Dropsus eat the pieces.

Be that as it may, some art historians interpret the Renaissance struggle for motion in art as an

Rubens' Apotheosis of St. Fidgeta
(RECONSTRUCTED)

attempt to depict St. Fidgeta. In Baroque art she received her best treatment, especially in the *Apotheosis of St. Fidgeta,* by Rubens, which was once the altarpiece of Santa Fidgeta in Tormento. The painting was hidden during the Allied invasion of Italy in World War II and is thought to be still camouflaged as a Coca-Cola sign.

Other famous representations are Caravaggio's *St. Fidgeta Chastised by St. Jerome* and Fragonard's *Saint Fidgeta in Ecstasy.*[2]

Miracles of St. Fidgeta

No account of this saint's life would be complete without mention of some of her more remarkable apparitions and miraculous feats. Most famous is the routing of the Turkish siege of Pinsk in 1450, when St. Fidgeta appeared as a fluffy pink cloud on the walls of the city and, stretching forth a chubby hand, induced in the heathen army a state of uneasiness that soon reduced the soldiers of the Prophet

---

[2] Professor Schlechty, in his *Fragonards Fidgetabild und Romantische Weltschmerz* (München, 1892), complains of the impropriety of having cupids pinching and tickling the saint. Sister Regina Coeli Laetare, O.F.F., in her *Fidgeta and the Problem of the Catholic Artist in an Altogether Too Secularized Society* (Altoona, 1932), retorts hotly that the cupids are allegorical.

Fragment of Fragonard

to nerveless idiocy.[3] In 658, the Persian Emperor Tissaphernes led his mighty host against the Byzantine city of Ud. But on the evening before a decisive battle, he retired to his tent with an unaccountable feeling of disquietude. He awoke in the night with a tiny voice in his ear saying "tickle, tickle" and soon was rolling on the ground in shrieking convulsions of laughter. His army fled in terror.

Naturally, there are many tales of miraculous cures attributed to St. Fidgeta. Children afflicted with incurable cases of diaper rash, itchy thumb, sweaty palms, and general fussing have been cured overnight when their distressed mothers prayed to the tiny saint. One such case is documented by a letter to the "Catholic Problems" column of the *Sunday Intruder:*

Dear Father Thurifer,

My six-year-old daughter Eudoxia was a chronic fidgeter. She twitched and fiddled endlessly during Mass, much to the consternation of myself and my husband Voltimand, who holds the consecutive Communions record at St. Ogmus Parish.

---

[3] It is thought that St. Fidgeta works on the Heavenly Host in a similar manner. St. Thomas says that she disrupts the order of the Angelic Hierarchy until her requests are granted. See *De Angelis.*

I tried everything to make her stop. I made ninety-two First Fridays, fifty-six First Saturdays, and twelve First Mondays, if there is such a thing, though I think my son Caxton made it up. I got callouses on my thumb from rosaries and sprained my index finger turning on electric vigil lights, even though Father Usk is stingy and turns them off every night. (Not that I mean any disrespect toward the clergy, of course. I just mean he knows a nickel when he sees one, ha, ha.) Anyway, I finally prayed to St. Fidgeta and my daughter stopped fidgeting. Once a week, though, she has what our family calls the screaming woo-hoos. Is there any saint for that?

Mrs. Emily Faldstool

Father Thurifer's answer, which need not be quoted in full here, indicates that the child's seizures are some variety of stigmata and should go away after a while.

Another letter from the *Intruder:*

Dear Father Plotch:

My son used to break into uncontrollable laughter during the Last Gospel. He says that one Sunday when this happened a little girl

2 3

with frizzy blond hair in the pew ahead of him said she would give him a fat lip if he didn't stop. After Mass we waited outside and no little blond girl came out! We think it was St. Fidgeta.

Mrs. Anthony Adverse Crapple

Finally, we ought to note the case of the little girl in the English village of Retching-under-Tweed who saw a mysterious light in the village chapel one night. She was not suffering from anything, nor did she ever see anything unusual again, but it was discovered that the chapel is only forty miles from the site of a medieval Fidgettine (or perhaps Ursuline) convent.

The St. Fidgeta Devotional

ST. ADIPOSA'S PRAYER FOR RELIEF FROM UNEASINESS (EFFECTIVE WITHIN TWENTY-FOUR HOURS):

O Sweet Fidgeta, tiniest candle on the sugar cake of Eternity, grant that my nervousness may be seared away by thy honeyed flame, or that it may at least be made useful, till I have passed through the stomach of life to . . .
(Here several words are blotted out, and the prayer seems never to have been finished.)

(TO BE CHANTED BY CHILDREN AGES 3-12)

Quieter of the giggly
Steadier of the wiggly

Teach us to sit still

Calmer of the tickly
Rubber of the prickly

From woolen shirts, squeaky corduroy and
metal laundry tags . . .

From the fear that also during the night the
can see our noses and that it will
make us cross-eyed . . .

From feet that go to sleep and will almost
certainly develop gangrene . . .

From the feeling that during the night we
will contract leprosy and our toes
will drop off and what will we do then . . .

Sweet Fidgeta,
deliver us!

From the unaccountable feeling that we
Communists will crawl over the window
sill and take over and will we have
the strength to die for our Faith . . .

From nuns who describe exactly what the
Indians did to St. Isaac Jogues and
his friends . . .

From demoniac possession, scabby knees, and
all causes of the desire to itch, twitch
or run screaming up and down . . .

O Fidgeta, who dost cause the unrighteous to scratch where it does not itch, grant that the hateful N. may be afflicted with tickles, the stitch, the cramp, underarm rash, prickly foot, and all manner of unexplained twinges.

II

PROLEGOMENON TO ANY FUTURE VISIT OF A POPE TO AMERICA

(Notes found in the desk of a New York advertising executive)

Next time it will be better. Haven't yet found the nun who was waving a Viet Cong flag. Paint the runway white and gold? Short Secret Service men in altar boy outfits with censers. Censers are smoke grenades in case of riot. Jesuits say they will lend their Aston-Martin for Pope, but I must check it first. Sign in Times Square with animated figure of Pope blessing people? Doubt if short-term rental fee would be worth it. Does open up a new field, though: "Paul Claudel smoked Gauloises"; "Thomas Merton says 'Buy Monks' Bread' "; "Jacques Maritain says 'Try Pepsi-Cola, the drink that *is*.' " Humpf. Znerb. Tweb. Canopy to hold over car would seem unwieldy. Poles have to be too long, and bearers would have to run like hell. Chair for Cardinal Spellman, carried by dwarves. Check skirts of drum majorettes for modesty. No novices with hula hoops. J. Edgar Hoover dressed up as Orthodox Patriarch.

27

A Pope in procession

His staff is machine gun. Pope stops in Harlem
again. Speech on how birth control is plot to destroy
the poor. Says he'd like to throw his tiara to the
crowd, but I am afraid it would hurt someone. Never
cared for the damn thing. Looks like something
you'd win at Coney Island. Like to hang it on top of
the Empire State Bldg. Go to whoever could climb
up and get it. Oh, well. Tickety-boo and Tyler too.
Tiddly-pom. Got to get him to loosen up a bit. Last
time he acted like something you'd carry through

the streets in an Italian village festival. Uncooked pizza has more expression. The press behaved well, though. Thank God Mencken is dead. I can hear him: "The Grand High Mucky-muck of the Italian Ghostly Trade came gallivanting into town today, followed by endless hordes of sweating beefy Irish priests and Polish dervishes from Toledo . . ." But everybody was nice: "A torrent of fervent emotion swept faithful Christian and hardened agnostic alike down the ageless turreted canyons of New York as the Pope rode serenely along, buoyed up on an airy cushion of good wishes." At the UN, even: "Crass atheists from the Iron Curtain countries, inscrutable Buddhists, sheeted Moslems—all queued up before the tiny man in the sugar-colored robe, whose gold-slippered foot rests lightly on the wills of the world's umpty-ump million Catholics." Great. And Buckley never carried out his threat to buy a block of seats in Yankee Stadium. Imagine a thousand people flashing cards spelling "Mater Si—Magistra No" during Mass. Says he would've done it if it had been John. Good thing John didn't come. The joke-cracking would've been okay, but he lacked what I may call the higher seriousness. Which, God knows, Paul does not lack. Tumpty-um-tum.

Biggest problem is the meeting with the President. Last one came off okay, though much squabbling about protocol. Monsignor Clute still thinks each one should've prostrated himself before a wax image of the other. The way I see it, we need the same shilly-shallying for weeks in advance. Neither thinks he's going to meet the other. Then about three days before P-day, the President decides to make a sudden impulsive visit to New York. Just to see if Central Park is still there. Then we have the confrontation. Say they both happen to stop into the Pan-Am Bldg. The routes might be like this:

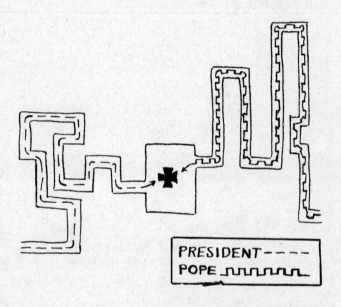

PRESIDENT - - - -
POPE ᴨᴨᴨᴨᴨ

They both come around the corner and bump into each other. Surprised as hell. After the usual amenities, we clear the flunkies out of the room so the

Byzantine icon of LBJ

President can drop his Shecks-a-mighty accent and
the Pope can stop using that "this humble person-
age" manner. They talk for a while about matters of
world importance, then exchange gifts. Who should
give who the cowboy boots? Could get a salt shaker
made like St. Peter's and one that looks like the
Capitol, but they'd get mixed up. A Byzantine icon
of LBJ? Holding motto: "Fear not. I have overcome
the world."

Mass at night in a blimp over Manhattan Island.
Maybe we can get them to blink the city lights at
the consecration.

III

THE CATHEDRAL OF ST. GORBODUC:

Volume I in the "Shrines That Live" Series

The Cathedral of St. Gorboduc (in Los Honchos, Spain) is one of the great examples of how many different styles of architecture may blend into a frozen fugue of harmonious integrity. St. Gorboduc's was finished in 1962, though it was begun in 623 under the Visigothic chieftain Harg. He was persuaded to build the church on the spot where he had (in his pre-Christian days) murdered his cousin Gorboduc. Harg's conversion was effected by the hermit Ulfag, who, to shame the chieftain, stood for forty days under the kitchen window of Harg's palace and was slowly buried by the garbage flung from that window. The holy man subsisted only on what food he could get when the garbage heap had reached the level of his mouth, and this spectacle softened the heart of Harg. The seventh century part of St. Gorboduc's is a low nave, six feet high, with twelve-foot-thick walls pierced here and there by round windows one foot in diameter. One gets

The hermit's strategem

33

from this part of the church a sense of massive strength.

No more work was done on the church until the thirteenth century, when the Abbot of Trocadero decided to build the first wooden Gothic church. Over the seventh century nave he threw up high Gothic arches of knotty pine and soaring mahogany buttresses, not to mention the cinquefoiled ogees, cross-purposed groining, crockets, finials, and imitation cane rood screen that mark this style as very early Diagonal.

All work stopped with the Horror of 1292, and nothing further was done till the Moorish conqueror Ishbar came to Los Honchos and converted the church into a mosque. He added the famous Salome Window (later painted over) and the Moorish interior, which is often compared with that of the Alhambra Theatre in South Bend, Indiana. When the church was repossessed by the Christians in 1491, the Gothic walls had begun to warp, splinter, and rot, so that the whole church had to be covered with a thick layer of pink stucco. In this period the bell tower was begun: it consists of four twenty-foot-high cherubs squatting in a circle, supporting a Buddha with a clock in its belly. The lotus blossom in the Buddha's navel goes in and out with the ticks of the clock.[1]

---

[1] The Buddha has been a puzzle to architectural historians for some time. "Perhaps it is merely a very fat cherub," sug-

The Chieftain Harg being observed
by the hermit Ulfag

In the eighteenth century, the French-born bishop Gruyère de la Bouche brought to St. Gorboduc's Deistic sermons and Greek Revival architecture. He is responsible for the Ionic colonnade surrounding the Buddha, and he tried to build a flat red brick roof for the church. Those who have attempted to lay bricks in a straight line across a void know the problems involved; but La Bouche refused to give up, and he strung up a wire mesh in which the bricks might be laid. Here he might have succeeded if his desire for novelty (which Pius IX has repeatedly warned us against) had not gotten the better of him again. The new baking powder mortar soon crumbled and today the bricks hang in the sagging wire screen like eggs in a basket.[2]

An architectural disaster

St. Gorboduc's church lay inchoate until the 1950s when a final drive was made to finish this historic fane. The pennies of Catholic school children gradually piled up on the desk of Whority and Sons, the famous Catholic architects of Babylon, Missouri, who undertook to complete what previous centuries had begun. They added two square glass towers, a corrugated steel roof, and some ferris-

gests Dr. Samp in his book *Some Puzzling Remnants* (Roachburg, 1903).

[2] "The bricks jostle and clunk dismally with every wind," points out Mrs. Ariel Hoagy in her article "Listening to Architecture," in *Plinth* (September, 1945).

36

Within the illustration:

ST. GORBODUC
MASSES: 6, 7, 8, 9, 10, 11, 12
1, 2, 3, 4, 5, 6, 7, 8, 9, 10, 11, 12
EAT MONKS BREAD

St. Gorboduc's Church

wheel flowerboxes that rotate with the wind. When the populace began to deride the towers, calling them "milk cartons," Arthur E. Whority issued a statement defending his company's aesthetics:

Of course our bold, new see-through towers look like milk cartons. We take our functionalized shapes from the things around us, like bread loaves, potato chip bags, and the like, just as Greek architects used acanthus leaves. This is an age of people on the go, so we like our shapes free, sharp, light, bright, and unencumbered with ornaments. We feel our towers belong to the world of young moderns: They are zippy, yet reverent.

The final fillip added by the Whority Company was a set of colored floodlights which bathe the church in the appropriate color for each liturgical season.

IV

THE QUESTION BOX

Q. Does the olive in the martini break the Lenten fast, or is it considered part of the drink?

A. This problem has vexed some of the subtlest minds of the Church. Is the olive *qua* olive part of the martini *qua* martini? Or is the olive a substance unto, of, and within itself, *per se* in the drink rather than *per accidens*? And the question is further complicated by the fact that, if we consider the composition of liquid matter, an electron is but a tiny olive afloat in the martini of the water glass (so to speak). But here the last word, as usual, goes to St. Thomas, who remarks in his *Summa Contra Omnes*: *"Oliva, quaecumque est, cibus est, et certe ieiunium frangit."* It must be pointed out here that St. Thomas had no mystical foreknowledge of the martini. He was merely listing those solids which are foods (as opposed to those which are not).

It must also be said here for the benefit of non-Catholic men who find themselves seated in bars next to Catholic young ladies during Lent, that the offer of an olive should not be construed as an attempt to establish an improper liaison.

Q. What about the cookie that is sometimes served with a malted?

A. Let us not be silly.

Q. Mrs. A. M. writes: What should I do about all the broken statues, worn-out prayerbooks, old Catholic calendars, and fragments of rosary beads that I have lying around? I know I shouldn't burn them and it doesn't seem right to bury them.

A. Save them. A modern home has lots of room. If you want to repair any of the statues, use Sacrosticky, a glue made from Lourdes water.

Q. Mrs. L. S. D. writes: Exactly what do I get if I make the five First Fridays? My son says that you get hauled off to heaven by some saint or other. And finally, what, if anything, is in the last Fatima letter?

A. In the first place, you have to make nine First Fridays. You don't get anything for five. In the second place, you seem to ask a lot of questions.

The Question Box Moderator

Q. Mr. Arthur "Dutch" Wolohan writes: My kids keep pestering me for money to ransom pagan babies. Who are we ransoming them from? If they're pagan, I'm not sure I want them.

A. Babies are only pagan because of their parents. If they are still pagan when they reach the age of reason, then they get wild and unruly. But we can save them and bring them up so they will be like the Catholic children in this country.

Q. Mrs. Annie Rugg writes: I have organized the biggest chain letter in the world. What are you going to do about it?

A. I don't have to do anything about it. You are a contemptible little old lady who probably draws chalk pentacles to summon up Guardian Angels. With all the devotions that exist in the Church, *you* have to pick one of the few that are universally condemned. And how do you *know* that your chain letter is the largest? Pride on top of superstition! Why don't you do something useful, like keeping a day-to-day record of all your good and bad deeds? Then when you die you'll have a rough idea of the state of your Eternal Ledger.

Q. Mrs. Septa Tanqueray writes: My children and I are freezing to death this winter because my husband claims that in his *Syllabus of Errors* Pius IX condemned the furnace as a modern invention. What can I do? P.S. We also grind our own grain for flour.

A. Come now. You can't be too frozen if you are able to write this letter, which I see is in a nice, firm (but feminine) hand. Stop whining and face up to your duty as a wife and mother. You might try electric blankets, which Pius IX didn't know about, although some theologians claim that we are bound by what a Pope is likely to have thought if he had lived long enough. See Father Bunty's book *Projected Thoughts of Popes*. Anyway, good for you for grinding your own flour.

Q. If an Anglican priest converts to Catholicism, are all the confessions he heard before his conversion invalid?

A. They are invalid even if he doesn't convert. The poor Anglican sinner that this "priest" has absolved is, sadly enough, like a man who thinks he has filled a book with enough green stamps for an Eternal Reward. When, on the Last Day, he comes to the Redemption Center, God looks at the book and hands it back, saying with a frown, "These are not my stamps. Go somewhere else." Still clutching his worthless scrip, the bilked penitent falls headlong down the crystal stairs, bumping his head all the way to the bottom.

Q. Miss Purina Sansfoy writes: I was out walking the other day in Chicago when I saw a lot of men tramping down the middle of the street. Each one was carrying a bowling ball, and the bowling balls were attached to each other by ropes. I guess it was a rosary of some kind. The men who were the Our Fathers had foghorns and were bellowing through them. The rest of the men said something in response. Behind them all came an Irish bagpipe band and a couple of men carrying a banner that said "Canonize Barry Fitzgerald." What do you suppose it all means?

A. I don't know. I checked the Bible, and it definitely is not a sign that the End is coming. Have you thought that it might all have been a hallucination brought on by excessive piety or by incense? Too much incense in a crowded damp church can produce odd effects, though since liturgical reform came in, incense poisoning has become a strictly Anglican disease. Perhaps you are an Anglican without knowing it.

Q. Mrs. Gertie Frem of Atropos, Kentucky, writes: Is it true that matzo crackers are made with Christian blood? And does the Schema on the Jews (or the Jewish Scheme, as my husband calls it) mean that I have to be nice to old Mr. Weintraub, who steals milk bottles off our back porch?

A. As for the first question, I would have to know the brand name. And to answer the second question I would have to know Mr. Weintraub.

Q. Benozzo Gozzoli of Tarentum, Pennsylvania, writes: I am fifteen, and every time I go to confession and confess unclean thoughts, the priest says "Think of baseball." I don't like baseball, though I do like hockey and pole-vaulting. But I am afraid that if I object I will seem stiff-necked and unrepentant. And I did try thinking of baseball, but it only made matters worse. Am I breaking the Seal of Confession by writing this letter?

A. Yes.

Q. Sister M. Fiorello writes: I teach Political Science at St. Gertrude-by-the-Tarn, and I want to use Marx's *Communist Manifesto* in a course. Not by itself, of course. I will use lots of other things that prove Marx is wrong. Well, I asked the Bishop for Index permission, and he said no. What do I do?

A. I don't think your students will be any worse off for not being able to read the perverted twaddle written by a Satanic old man with a big bushy beard. Remember that the bad tree cannot bear good fruit. I used to teach a course in Atheistic Communism, and I always found that Bishop Sheen's book satisfied my needs.

45

Q. "Aunt Min" writes: My mother-in-law is eighty-nine and lives in the front hallway. Since she is the first thing our guests see when they come in the front door, we don't have many friends left, and they come around to the back door. And she is always edging her rocker over to the foot of the staircase, so that people can't get up or down the stairs. I would like to poison the old hag. Is there any way of doing it without violating the Fifth Commandment?

A. Use the Principle of Double Intent: (1) You *do* want her out of the way, and (2) you *don't* want to be guilty of murder. For this solution you must thank the great casuist, Father B. U. Gormless, S.J., who discovered the Principle of Double Intent in 1952. It is discussed at length in his book *Mental Reservations and Other Traps* (Cuminseed Press).

Q. Father Burgerbitz of St. Lintel's Abbey writes: The other day when I was teaching Redemptive Transmigration I, a student asked me this question: "Since Christ and the Blessed Virgin are in Heaven bodily, and since body implies place, then Heaven must be in *some* place. What if our spaceships fly into it by mistake?" I have been ransacking the library and phoning observatories, but I can't find an answer. What do you say?

A. Your student's theology is correct, but he is lacking in the virtue of Hope. If Flash Gordon, a fictional hero, can shoot down spaceships, then God certainly can.

Q. Mrs. Modine Clapp writes: For twenty-five years now, my mother and I have had the same pew in St. Frognall and Companions Church. Well, every Sunday this old rep who married out of the Church in 1920 comes and sits in front of us. When he tries to get up and go to Communion, my mother hooks her cane around his adam's apple and chokes off his wind till he gets tired and gives up. Lately he has tried sitting in other pews, but we have followed him. Last week he broke his collarbone, and so he is wearing a big high brace that my mother's cane won't fit around. Should we tunk him on the head?

A. It would probably cause too much of a commotion. Most people who are tunked go "uhhh" and slump over forward, thus attracting attention. Those who see all this but do not know the full story will condemn your action, though from what you have told me, the folks in your parish don't notice much. At the very least, they will think he has had a heart attack, and what with all the doctors and ambulances and Last Rites, you will wish you had never started anything. I think you will find that a little anonymous telephone harassment is worth a world of choking and clubbing. And you can get your old pew back.

Q. My name is Becky May Tipover and I hav seen a boy in my Cathlic grade school going to a YMCA Chrismas party. I turned him in to Sister Oza and she giv him a good balling out and I laft and sed servs you rite dopy it ses in the Catty Cism that we shoud avoid ocassons of sin and he sed your a fink Ile steel all the vidgel lites in the church and rost you over a sloe fier. I screemd and the big sister who is alwais braging about her mussels cam and giv it to him agen. And now he sets behind me an wispers I cen cut yor throt with a ruler and not lev a traice. What should I do?

A. My dear child: you acted rightly in the first place by heading off the boy's tendency toward wispy, wavery, watered-down Catholicism. Any punishment he metes out to you will be rained tenfold upon his head in the Afterlife, not to mention what he will get in this life from the sister with the muscles. But I don't think he can cut your throat with a ruler, even one with a little metal edge on it, and in any case traces *will* be left. If he does murder you, emulate St. Maria Goretti by forgiving him, preferably with your last breath.

Q. I. H. Samsonite writes: My eighteen-year-old-son, although he is going to a Catholic college, subscribes to the *Catholic Worker,* which comes to our house without even a plain brown wrapper. He goes to pacifist meetings and wears a button that says "Dean Husk is made out of library paste." And last week I caught him trying to peel the "Get Out of the UN" sign off the bumper of our car. He claims that the Pope endorsed the UN by his visit. Is this true?

A. Of course not. If you read the right Catholic papers (and you might pass them on to your son) you will see letters and articles that prove conclusively that the Pope came to the UN to shake the secular nations out of their indifferentist, left-wing torpor. The UN was the only place where he could find the representatives of all those nations gathered together. As for your son's pacifism, the very idea of a Catholic pacifist is ridiculous. Look at the Crusades. Look at Catholic France under Napoleon. Look at the abbot who was besieging an Albigensian town which had some Catholics in it. When asked who should be burned, he said, "Kill them all.

God will take care of his own." Mention Catholic pacifism to any army officer, and he will laugh. Mention it to a Catholic mother whose son is in Viet Nam, and she will hit you. Tell your son to form a devotion to some saint who was a soldier. And who, may I ask, is Dean Husk?

V

A SHORT GUIDE TO CATHOLIC CHURCH HISTORY FOR CATHOLIC COLLEGE STUDENTS GOING OUT INTO THE WORLD TO DEFEND THEIR FAITH

Omnis Obstat: Orcus Cardinal Bugloss, Bishop of
   Ravenna (Ga.)

Nemo Me Impune Lacessit: Thomas O'Hogarty
   Gormenghast, Lictor Magnificus

There are only a few things the well-informed Catholic absolutely *must* know about Church history. These are:

1. Popes
   a. Good
   b. Bad
   c. Lost
2. Schisms
3. Heresies
4. Old Canards

Popes

Since no Catholic will be called upon to defend Good Popes, and since we know nothing at all about the Lost Popes, let us concentrate upon Bad Popes.

The worst Pontiff ever to slouch menacingly in a corner of the Chair of Peter was Spatulus III (898–899), who came to power as the nerveless ninth century was dissolving imperceptibly into the tepid tenth. He was, no doubt, a product of his times, born to a family of decayed Roman nobility in an age when Rome was little more than Khayyam's "battered caravanserai." To be fair, we must say that Spatulus might have been better if his mother Papella had not kept him in a root cellar from the time he was three till his election at forty-two. As it turned out, he was (to quote the learned Father Roodscreed) "no better and no worse than one might expect."

Reasons for Spatulus' decadence

Among the more interesting excesses of Pope Spatulus were:

a) His love of rock candy. He made a little house out of it in the garden of his villa at Spumanti and took his mistresses there for unspeakable rites.

b) His dog Gorgo. "It was much too large," says Father Grabney in his book *The Dog at Rome: Famous Pets of Popes*.

c) His insistence on dressing up as Amun-Ra and his fortunately averted scheme to be declared an Egyptian divinity.

Spatulus was crushed to death by the Curia in 899 after making six necrophiles and a hat fetishist cardinals.

The worst Renaissance Pope was Bragghimento dei Crudelissimi, who took the name of Sporus VI (1540–1565). His election took place under most peculiar circumstances, since the Curia in 1540 had been drastically reduced by plague, sudden death, and a drowsy euphoria that came drifting up out of the Pontine Marshes like the exhalations of some besotted giant. At Sporus' election, fifteen prelates were present, with an average age of eighty-six. Eight were certainly senile, and there may be some question about Balbo of Genoa, who kept spilling his ink during the balloting, and who constantly referred to the cardinal next to him as "Rosa." The fifteenth ballot had been reached when a disturbance arose over pens. Old Cardinal Schotto of Mainz had broken his and could not secure another from the proctors, whom he accused (loudly) of being in the pay of the Italians. He advanced to the middle of the room, denouncing violently, and was met by three proctors, two Italian cardinals, and Scataphorus, the ninety-eight-year-old Patriarch of Alexandria, who was trying (in a general way) to find the bathroom. The scene that followed is recorded

A disturbance over pens

53

by an English recusant cardinal, to whose account we shall now turn:

The olde Germayne Cardinall did then seaze a seruing boye by the scruffe of the necke and did crye (Heere I traunslate the Latyn tonge) "Hoe, turvy-arse, where bee thy pennes?" "Gramercy, Signor," quod the boye, "but I haue nonne." Whereat the cardinall did hale hym upp & downe, callyng hym toadie, snott-nose, and divers thinges too corse for trauns-scripture, vntill the Italique Cardinalls did praye hym leaue offe. Hee thenn turnd on them wyth a cric, and begannc to belabour them bothe with hys crozyer, showtyng "Woulde ye soe? Eh? Ha?" The twoe bare hym to the grownde in a tryce, and pummeld hym, til hee did crye "Mercie, noble Signors, for I ment it butt a jeste." Heere an olde Greekish Signor approchd and beganne to butt the Lord Schot-toes hed wyth hys staffe, takyng it for the floore. Whereon hee whych lay prone layd holde on the Greeke lordes beerd, and puld hym downe in a pyle with the other three. And att thys suche a clamour wente vp as wolde haue affrighted a herde of Chymaeras, with cryes of "You spitt in my face, & Ile spitt in yores," "Holde off, Brushe-face," and soe on. A boye came vnto mee & tugd at my mantel,

The election of Pope Sporus VI

sayeing "Hoe, milorde, wouldst helpe vs pull them aparte?" "Bumbastrills, puffpasties, and rotten figges to ye all," says I, & heere I left.

After this unseemly tiff, the balloting proceeded, though Cardinal Schotto never did get a pen, and afterward boasted that he had marked his ballot with soot from the Greek patriarch's beard.

Sporus was elected and immediately acknowledged three mistresses, a concubine, and fourteen illegitimate children, supporting this move with his campaign slogan, "Honesty in the Church." But honesty was not enough, for he was, alas, prone to bribery, nepotism, and murder, and his reign was thus pockmarked by many scandals. Not the least of these incidents was the series of attempts he and Cardinal Bobbo made to poison each other. The

A jar of tainted quinces

latter sent Pope Sporus a jar of tainted quinces, which were (fortunately) devoured by one of the Pope's greedy nephews. Sporus responded with a lute filled with tarantulas, which was accompanied by a gaily mocking note in classical Greek hexameters. The cardinal shot back with a music box which, when opened, played early Renaissance airs as it fired a small phial of bat saliva at the unlucky recipient. Sporus, however, ended the tomfoolery in a rather crude manner, when he invited Cardinal Bobbo to a card party and threw him down a well.

It must not be forgotten, however, that Pope Sporus VI was a patron of the arts. Up until 1921, one could see near Rome some traces of the Villa Pasta, which Sporus built from the ruins of twenty-five old Roman temples in the vicinity. Furthermore, he was the patron of Sandro di Garagiola, who did the famous, if fanciful, frescoes entitled "Pope Sporus Debating with Aristotle," "Pope Sporus Duelling with the Spirits of Nestorius and John Hus," and "Pope Sporus Being Begged by the Curia Not To Abdicate and Go To Live on Patmos as a Hermit."

But not even art could preserve Pope Sporus from the recurrent attacks of *mal de siècle* that sent him, in the twilight of his reign, more and more frequently to Capri. Though he was unsuccessful in establishing that island as the summer residence of the Popes, he became a legend there. The islanders still talk of the way he would wander about in brightly flowered robes, leather sandals, and a straw tiara he had had made for him.[1] At last, in October of 1565, this unhappy man was called before that cloudy Bar of Justice on which no earthly gavel can ring. He was blown off Tiberius' Leap during a high wind and was drowned.

Sporus' tragic decline

---

[1] Some virulently anti-Catholic historians insist that Pope Sporus wore smoked spectacles with this costume. This is nonsense.

Things to Remember: The thing to remember about these "Bad" Popes is that they proclaimed no *ex cathedra* doctrines.

Schisms

Only one schism is really important, and that is the Grand Central Schism. It started on a muggy afternoon in August of 1252, when a dispute broke out in Rome between French and German cardinals. The former claimed that the latter had taken over the kitchen facilities at the conclave they were attending, and that fifteen straight meals of bratwurst, beer, and sauerkraut were affecting their minds. The Germans laughed the protest off and took to singing *"Frère Jacques"* in thin piping voices under the French cardinals' windows at 3 A.M. Relations gradually worsened, and soon the French faction left Rome, amid cries of *"Pah!"* and *"Droit sans honneur!"* They fled to the French cathedral town of Oeufs, where they elected the antipope Carius. The events that followed, because of their complexity, we shall give in the form of a historical outline:

October, 1252: Four French cardinals on their way from Oeufs to Rome with a bull of excommunication stop at a wayside inn near Pisa, where they meet four Italian cardinals who are merely vacationing. Three days later, they all elect Phobus IV.

Sauerkraut leads to break

November, 1252: The Turkish pirate Ragbash seizes the Dalmatian port of Spug and threatens to impale the populace if they do not make him Pope. He is elected by acclamation.

December, 1252: The Popes exchange excommunications for Christmas.

January, 1253: The Dutch mystic Jan ter Koot claims that he knows who the real Pope is. No one seems interested.

May, 1253: All claimants to the Papal throne meet in the old Roman amphitheatre at Verona. All agree on Zosimus II, except the Turkish claimant, who retires to a small island in the Adriatic, where he re-elects himself from time to time over the years.

January, 1254: Four men claiming to be antipopes appear in a boat on the Tiber. They disappear completely.

Heresies

The Church has often been plagued by the gnats of heresy, which have sometimes lain on her shores "thick as autumnal leaves that strow the brooks in Vallombrosa." No heresies exist today, though some unfortunate differences of opinion do. Some of the more interesting ancient heresies you should know about are:

The Monophonic Heresy. This was the belief that

the Heavenly Host sings with one voice and not with many hierarchically arranged voices. In silencing the adherents of this doctrine, Sector of Rheims (called "The Flawless Thinker") asked them what that voice sounded like. They could not tell him.

The Econophanic Heresy. Followers of this aberrant fantasy claimed that there was, in addition to the Treasure House of Grace, a Treasure House of Sin, drawn on by the Devil and his angels. They elaborated this system to include demonic comptrollers, tellers, guards, and vice presidents. It was not long before this sect became explicitly demonic, as Econophanes went about waving checks drawn on their hellish accounts, and claiming that Satan gave higher interest rates. Fortunately, the whole movement collapsed when word got around that a run on the bank had occurred. The Econophanes were found sitting on curbstones or stumbling aimlessly along, their faces those of ruined men.

The Scrupularian Heresy. This doctrine arose from the ticklish question first asked by the fifteenth century proto-seminalist, Orduri della Vacca: Is one sin repeated all day long one big sin or many tiny ones? His disciple Pedasculus claimed that, since time is infinitely divisible and subdivisible, there are as many sins as there are moments of time. Since not many people are willing to confess an infinite number of sins, the heresy has remained con-

Ganymede V gamboling in his garden and being observed by Leonardo

fined to its originator. The logical basis for this view has never been formally proved wrong, though Father Widdershins, O.P., the noted Thomist, claims that the answer will be forthcoming now that his Casuistry Institute has an electronic syllogism machine with a self-winding dialectic.

Old Canards

The Pope Joan Story. Some foolish people believe that there was once a female Pope who was elected by mistake. This story probably originated several years after the papacy of Ganymede V, a Pope of doubtful masculinity. This golden-haired, rather limp-wristed young man was elected in 1503, after an unusually long run of lecherous Popes; the feeling was that he would reverse the trend. The chronically anti-Catholic historian Furze calls Ganymede "a raving queen," but that indelicate epithet is unkindly used against this admittedly confused man, who had a habit of fainting into the arms of Leonardo da Vinci. It is true, of course, that the great Leonardo's unfinished painting "Saint Sebastian Dying in a Bed of Zinnias" was inspired by the sight of Ganymede running through the Boboli Gardens, clad only in a kirtle of begonias. But all rumors, true or otherwise, should have stopped when Ganymede was found dead in his bed one summer day in 1505. He had been smothered by orchids, which were poured into the room through the skylight while he slept.

The Galileo Story. Everybody thinks that Galileo was imprisoned by the Inquisition for claiming that the earth moves around the sun. But it wasn't that at all. Galileo just didn't have much proof for what he was saying, and the Church from that day to this has been opposed to the spirit of irresponsible criticism. Besides, we know now that there *is* a sense in which the sun moves around the earth, since everything is in motion and is therefore relative (except morality and the authority of the Church).

The Tunnel from the Vatican to the White House. This old tale got started when Gov. Alfred Smith ran for President in 1928. No reasonable person could possibly believe it. On the other hand, there is good reason to believe that there is a tunnel between the Kremlin and the Washington office of the American Civil Liberties Union.

VI

A FABLE OF GOAR

A FABLE OF GOAR

Once long ago in Germany there lived a Saint named Goar...

He ran a ferry boat on the Rhine, and when he reached the middle of the river, he always asked the same question.

EVENTUALLY WORD OF GOAR'S ZEAL GOT TO THE BISHOP.

SO EVERYONE WENT DOWN TO THE RHINE TO FIND ST. GOAR.
THE END.

VII

EASTER ADDRESS TO THE FACULTY BY THE PRESIDENT OF A CATHOLIC WOMEN'S COLLEGE

[SETTING: *A College Study somewhere in eastern Montana. The coffered gold-leaf ceiling is twenty-five feet high and is supported by columns of jasper, onyx, and lapis lazuli. On one side of the room is a row of fifteen-foot-high windows, which have wavy glass panes and heavy mahogany sashes. For that matter, all the woodwork in the room, including the head-high wainscot and the hand-carved door-frames, is mahogany, and all of it is polished to a blinding luster. The floor, also highly polished, is ebony parquet, interlaced with squares of ivory in a chessboard pattern. At one end of the room is a three-level dais: the topmost level supports a green soapstone chair, which in turn supports the Mother General of the Order. On the second level are the sisters of the Board of Governors, in medieval choir stalls. On the lowest level is a carved lectern, and behind it stands the President, Sister Justinian, who is about to address the faculty, lay, and religious, who are seated before her in chairs which range in style from Louis XIV to General Grant. Around the sides of the room are long Victorian library tables, which are being polished by an old, stooped-over nun. She continues to polish all through the speech.*]

The Address

Esteemed Mother, Honored Sisters, Reverend Fathers, and lay faculty. I call you together at this joyful time to discuss several pressing matters which have been placed in my lap. Things have a way of coming to my attention around here [*laughter among some of the nuns*].

In the first place, it seems that some of you have objected to the fact that Sister Coroda, the head of the Chemistry Department, has taken up the entire third floor of the new Science Hall with her office, bakery, candy store, and private TV lounge. Some of you have even tried to persuade Sister Visual Aids . . . excuse me . . . Sister Jeuna, to make Sister Coroda return the three tape recorders and two projectors she has out. [*With cold fury*] It may interest you to know that she is using this equipment to record TV shows for use in homes for the mentally retarded. It may also interest you to know that Sister

The President addressing her faculty

Coroda's fifty years of service here have given her the *ius primae usufructus* on all college equipment.

Secondly, I wish to announce that we are having . . . um . . . chest supports and pantalettas painted on the two Cubist nudes in the art gallery—that is, as soon as we find out what goes where [*she laughs*]. I have never seemed prudish to myself, but I think those paintings do not correspond to Sister Mavra's definition of Christian art as art created by a Christian artist while he is in a state of grace. And while we are on the Art Department, I might say that I was shocked when I wandered into Mr. Sago's drawing class and found a live female model clad only in a transparent raincoat. Black rubber mackintoshes will be used after this. [*Professor Eiger of the Psychology Department raises his hand, but she ignores him.*]

Another thing has been bothering me lately. I have heard the usual neurotic complainers whining because I keep the light bulbs, the school pencils, and the keys to the School Car in my office. Well, if I were to hire someone to look after such things, it would lower the salaries of some people I know. A few of you have taught classes in the dark just to be funny, but I'm afraid I don't see the joke.

On a more pleasant subject, I might say that we have been loosening up the rules a bit around here, despite the determination of some of you to think of me as an old mossy wimple. Next September we will have an agnostic teaching Home Economics here, and next year students over twenty-one may drink at home, provided their parents are present. Finally, for you impatient men, there is now a powder room for your use. It is in the home of Mr. and Mrs. Charles Dudmer of 1821 Peavy St.

And now a few brief announcements. I see many of you looking around for Professor Gargan of the English Department. You do not see him. There is a good reason for that: His tenure has been adjusted. [*A stir*] But I wouldn't worry, since he can live off the royalties from his new novel. I believe it is called *Twilight of the Gonads*.

I also want to tell you that next year's recipient of our Patriotism Award is Chiang Kai-Shek. It is hoped that he will be able to make it here to receive the award in person. Last year, you will remember, Professor Reichsmotif, the discoverer of synthetic yaws, was kept at home by a nearly fatal illness.

Finally—and I have been saving this news for last—the Mother General wishes me to tell you that an unprecedented number of our sisters have gotten doctorates in the past year. There are enough, in fact, to replace all the lay faculty, whom we are releasing as of June 1. I'm sure you will all find positions equal to your worth, whatever that may be. God bless you all and best wishes for a Blissful and Blessed Easter.

VIII

THE STORY OF ST. FLORADORA

St. Floradora's strange story begins in a pile of rubble at Pompeii. In this formless jumble were found some lettered tiles which somehow seemed to magically arrange themselves into the name FLORADORA. The stunned archaeologists rushed to the local priests, who immediately proclaimed that a martyr's tomb had been found. This interpretation of the cryptic tiles was corroborated by the discovery of a skeleton nearby. The skeleton, certainly female, was found in a crouching position, and it clutched to its spindly breast a moldered leather bag of coins. From this evidence it was assumed that Floradora, doubtless the Christian daughter of a vacationing Roman senator, had come to scatter coins in the streets for the poor and had been forced to take cover during the fatal eruption. Father Tumpline, the great popular hagiographer, reconstructs the scene for us in his *Floradora: Lines Writ in Lava:*

Forced to hide during the eruption

77

We see Floradora. her glossy aureate curls shining in the crisp Italian sunlight, scattering the tinkling denarii while the ragged children grovel for them amid thankful cries. Suddenly overhead an awful pall of sulphurous cloud spreads its stenchy mantle, and Floradora rushes into a nearby basement for cover, little dreaming that her dusty sojourn amid the ashes and pumice would last till Gabriel's trump.

This discovery was made in 1880, and by 1940 the landscape of the Catholic World was dotted with convents, churches, grade schools, and nuns named for St. Floradora, the Pompeiian Rose. Who has not heard of Sister M. Floradora, A.R.G., the talented poetess who teaches English at St. Sandra's College in Shoat, Iowa? Her. quicksilver pen gave us the "Lament for St. Floradora," which was, by her own admission, "written in the style of the great Catholic poet, Alexander Pope."

Lament for St. Floradora
(SPOKEN BY A RUDE SWAIN)
I stand amidst the frost-bit grain
And smite my oaten lyre again:
The cragful mont, the shaggish dale,
The bank o'erhung with kelp and kale,

St. Floradora

The croaky pond with froggy thrum,
O'ercrusted, and with healthless scum;
The dinky[1] grot, the sluggy stream,
The welkin fraught with birdy scream,
All echo back *Flor'dora's* name;
Slugs lisp it, though their meter's lame.
Soon winter falls: the verdant plot,
With glacial scunge is overwrought.
Hibernus, snudging o'er the glebe[2]
Puts bugs to flight, and eke the grebe.
His coldish craw to—here I stopp'd.
And on my foot my lute I dropp'd.

For *Clorabel,* my shepherd maid,
Had noiseless slipped through corny glade,
And in my ear she softly say'd:
Omit thy rue and stanch thy weeps,
And dry thine eyes with sottish sedge.
Thy *Florador* no longer sleeps,
But o'er the clouds trims heaven's hedge.
She mucks about in useful toil

---

[1] Dr. Bustard, writing in *The Compositor* (June, 1935), points out that Sister Floradora almost certainly wrote "inky" here. He blames the error on a roguish typesetter. Sister Floradora, however, in her letter to *The Compositor* (December, 1935), says: "If I had meant to write 'inky,' I would have written it."

[2] The author supplies this gloss on the line: " 'Snudge' means 'miser.' I imagine Winter crawling over the field on all fours, like a miser looking for lost coins."

Till God the pot brings to a boil.[3]
Then we, like carrots in a stew
Shall mingle in a Heav'nly Brew.

The Floradorine bandwagon thus rolled on un-
impeded till it was given its first jolt by the scholarly
potholes of Professor T. Oates Frostauger of Cam-
bridge who was in 1939 Hercules Furens Visiting
Lecturer at the University of the Funicular, near
Ostia. His article in the June 1940 issue of *Sherds*
("Some Calm Observations on a Few Lettered Tiles
and Old Bones") charged—albeit in a cool, distant
tone—that the Pompeiian basement where St. Floradora's bones were found had, in fact, been part of
a brothel. "This," commented the professor, "puts a
somewhat different interpretation on the money-
bag." Furthermore, he claimed that the lettered tiles
were only part of an inscription which, when intact,
read   FL[AVIVS]   OR[GVLVS]   ADORA[T]
[PVELLAM].

All the copies of this particular issue of *Sherds*
were bought up by Father Crostaciano, Rector
Tranquillus of Rome's Instituto Superbo, who hid
them in the storeroom of the Vatican Library. But

*Scholarly
potholes*

---

[3] "This line is dangerously close to blasphemy," writes Mrs.
Elda Shamprey in her letter to the editors of *Kerygmagazine*.
"And if it is an attempt to mock our corpulent clergy (Sister
Flora should know better), it wholly misses the point."

in 1949, the magazines were found in some baled waste paper which was being sent to a convent which makes *papier-mâché* fig leaves for statues in the Vatican Museum. Now the winds of controversy were out of the bag, and a scholarly tempest roared across Europe. Étienne Mougir's scathing article *"Seinte—Ha!"* was answered by Oswald Preiselbeersaft's triumphant *"Heilige—Ja!"* Dr. Plitheroe's searching article "The Brothel as Sanctuary" (*Plethora,* Winter 1950) called forth Dr. Frostauger's stinging attack "How Would *You* Know?," an open letter printed in *TLS*.

Finally, the problem was investigated by the Secretariat on Saintliness, which worked on the matter in secrecy for years. Informed sources differed about what was going on behind the nail-studded doors at 68 Via Caligula. For instance, *Time's* report ran thus (in part):

> Short, fat, bulb-nosed Father Wisney twiddled his beads on the Janiculum and sniveled, "You'll find out soon enough." Obnoxious Bishop Corvo raved, "Newsmen are the vomit of the secular world!" Intoned a cardinal wheezing up the Spanish Steps, "As far as I'm concerned, Floradora was a floozie." But an Italian-born housewife in Trenton, New Jersey, sobbed, "My husband built a statue of St. Floradora out of seashells. It's in our back yard and

the kids love it." And the Pope, sitting up in bed in the pre-dawn darkness, muttered, "What kind of name is Frostauger, anyway?"

On the other hand, *L'Osservatore Romano* said:
As we have it from the holy lips, the martyr's crown will not be wrenched from the glorious head of St. Floradora without further consideration. The experts, whose brows conceal libraries of specialized and sacred knowledge, will decide the matter in God's own sweet time. Meanwhile, let there be no street-corner haggling, no millwheel clatter of uninformed tongues. When the bronze portals of information swing wide on authoritative hinges, we will listen, and we will obey.

In 1959, the name of St. Floradora was silently dropped from the Roll of Saints, but the pandemonium that followed this decision was far from silent. Roving bands of iconoclasts were seen in many parishes, and many a pastor was jolted out of his bed at night by the clunk of steel against plaster. Embittered Irish Catholics razed the Shrine of St. Floradora at Ballyspitteen and used the rubble to derail the night train from Belfast. And in Chicago, the twelve churches named for the now disgraced saint were hastily rededicated to St. Nymphadota, a third-century ascetic from Leptis Magna who lived

Roving bands of iconoclasts

83

for thirty years in a hollow tree, subsisting on a diet of deathwatch beetles.

But the saddest fate of all befell Sister Floradora, the previously mentioned poetess, who began to act strangely after the fatal pronouncement. She somehow formed the idea that she must follow her namesake, no matter what, and she was found one day standing dazed under a lamppost, carrying a pair of black net stockings. Eventually, a noted theologian convinced her that, since the name "Floradora" was itself a fraud, she was not obliged to follow the career of a nameless Pompeiian courtesan. She is now Sister Dido, and is in good mental shape, except for occasional delusions of lubricity.

Upon the case of the Little Order of Floradora of Baines, Oregon—all of whose members moved to Montmartre—it would not be seemly to dwell. But amid all the clamor of renaming and wrecking, one question kept popping up: What happened to the prayers addressed to this nonexistent saint? "They were probably picked up by some saint or other," comments Father Barbican in *Orb*.

Sister Floradora, dazed

IX

LETTER FROM VATICAN CITY

by Nepomuk Prynne

September 14, 1985

This morning, as brightly painted banners decked the marmoreal breast of St. Peter's Basilica (the old festooned by the new), the fourth and most crucial session of Vatican III got under way. From our post high atop Bernini's colonnade, we watched with awe the solemn parade of bishops trooping into the great church, and we spotted several of the prelates who have made their presence felt here. One was Charles ("Buzzy") Cardinal Sparber, the thirty-five-year-old "boy wonder" Archbishop of Los Angeles. After breezing through Catholic University for his A.B., M.A., and S.T.D. degrees, young Father Sparber became national chaplain of the YAF and led the fight to ban the sale of Bulgarian wheat pilaf in California. His sponsorship of responsible conservative causes quickly made him a monsignor, and it was but a short step from there to the palm-shaded

Charles ("Buzzy") Cardinal Sparber

episcopal throne of the City of Angels. He has already caused quite a stir at this Council by contesting the presence of Russian Orthodox observers, and by wearing a dark blue cope covered with little white stars. The cope is decorated with orphreys depicting scenes from the American Revolution.

We also saw Cardinal Posidonio Spulci of Spoleto, who electrified the third session of the Council with his plan to make artificial Birth Control a Venial Sin. One of fourteen recently created Italian cardinals, he is considered a "liberal," though we know that "liberal" and "conservative" are terms that have little meaning for men who are merely doing the simple work of God.

Then there was Archbishop Ercolaneo Clotto-vecchio, the Apostolic Delegate to the United States, who recently put the American laity under a ban of *dulcissimus*. "This ban," explained Monsignor Gobart (one of the *periti* at the Council), "means that American Catholics, especially the self-styled liberals, must be as sweet and understanding as possible in the future. They must not carp about the decrees of the Council or engage in the kind of irresponsible criticism that has in the past confused the faithful." In connection with this decree, Archbishop Clottovecchio revealed before the last session his concept of the Church Dormant. "The Church Dormant," Monsignor Gobart pointed out, "is what those more rambunctious members of the Church should become. The Archbishop has demonstrated that it might be prudent—indeed, necessary—for those Catholics with overactive imaginations and chronic doubts to go into a sort of spiritual hibernation, to merely (in the Archbishop's words) 'sit tight' till the Day of Judgment."

Yesterday two huge trucks rolled into Vatican City with a matched pair of gleaming new ICBM's recently donated by an American bishop. The rockets are white and gold; their nose cones are shaped like papal tiaras; and they are tipped with double-barred papal crosses. Soon they will stand like twin monitory fingers near their newly built imitation Baroque control bunker. Despite the outcry from some of the more scrupulous Council fathers, especially those who voted to condemn nuclear arms at the last Vatican Council, the rockets seemed morally unimpeachable to most old Curia hands. After all, they are only tipped with dynamite. "And they will probably never be used, anyway," said a high Vatican source, "though their presence will add immeasurably to the power and majesty of the Church. Best of all, they are the perfect squelch to Stalin's crack about how many divisions the Pope has."

Speaking of the Pope, he has just returned from a visit to Andorra (he is the first Pope ever to visit Andorra) and is expected to comment on the limited nuclear war now raging in Southeast Asia. The accidental atomizing of Greenland last year called forth the encyclical *Sistite Si Vobis Placet* (Please Stop), but this year's encyclical crop has produced only *Et Antiquum Documentum,* which shows that many supposed errors of the Greek and Latin Fathers are in reality cleverly concealed truths.

The Pope will probably report tomorrow on his trip last fall to several Catholic colleges in the U.S.

Bishops on their way to a Council Session

His secretary, Father Cordwain, informs us that the trip was not all the Pope had expected it to be, since in every instance the college he visited had sent all its lay students home and had filled the dormitories with nuns, priests, and brothers. At the time of the visitation, Sandy Pylos, Student Body President of Mt. Athos College in Corfu, New York, sent to the Vatican a bitter protest signed by two thousand members of the National Catholic Student Synod (NACSTUS). The Holy Office, after due consideration, issued a *bulla oblongata* entitled *Nil Inultum Remanebit,* which in effect placed NACSTUS under interdict. We talked about this matter with Father Wampyir, Praetor of Mt. Athos College, whom we found studying the exhibit of ancient chains in the Church of San Pietro in Vincoli. "Those kids deserved whatever they got," commented Father Wampyir. "They read Joyce and neglect Chesterton and Belloc; they picket chanceries but not birth control clinics; and now they want to do a lot of poor nuns and brothers out of a chance to see their Spiritual Leader. Those students have enough money to come to Rome for an audience. If they didn't have the shekels, they sure as hell wouldn't be in Catholic colleges." We both laughed at this and went off together to visit the tomb of Pius XII.

This little collegiate quarrel will be no more than a ripple on the placid surface of this Council, whose waters overspread the filthy mantled pool of secularism. Today the Commission on Marian Titles will read a list of all possible Marian titles, and the fathers will indicate approval or disapproval by waving a lily. The unpruned list, printed in uncials on a parchment scroll, was yesterday laid out in its full length for the benefit of *Life* photographers. It stretched from the altar rail of St. Peter's to the house of Mr. and Mrs. Arthur Sims, 38 Via Pulcinella.

Later this month, the Council will tackle the Schema on the Index, which calls for drastic revision of this musty leftover from the Counter-reformation days. According to the new plan, certain approved presses will issue deluxe folio editions of Indexed books, done in elegant black-letter type and bound in full crumbled mauve levant morocco (top edges gilt). Half of each book will be a refutation of the book's errors by a prominent Catholic theologian. These editions will be on sale only in the bookstores of Catholic colleges, which will stock the books in no other form. In this way, Catholic college libraries will be able to get rid of all the cumbersome grilles, cages, steel rooms, and cyclone-fenced enclosures that now take up so much space. Accidental electrocutions will be only a disturbing memory.

It is hoped that this session will not see incidents like those which marred the spring session. Everyone here still remembers the case of the elderly American bishop who, during the debate on the Baltimore Catechism as a possible third source of Revelation, got the idea that a nuclear cataclysm had occurred in Baltimore. He rose to his feet, demanded the floor, and mystified the Council with an hour-long harangue against godless Communism. And there

93

Bishop of South Saigon,
Puppet Emperor of Manchuria

was the problem created by the Bishop of South
Saigon, who found out during March that the CIA
had made him Puppet Emperor of Manchuria. For
the rest of the session he behaved in a surly and
overbearing manner, and created some nasty problems of precedence, though he finally stopped coming to the Council under a gilt parasol.

But the worst squabble of all involved Bishop
Ratkissonescu, Prelate Numquam of Rumania, who
wandered off during one of the Council's dull mo-

ments to find the bathroom of Cardinal Bibbiena.[1] The prelate, tapping at walls with his staff and occasionally dislodging a bit of plaster, was apprehended by two Swiss guards, who held him incommunicado for six hours in an unused nuns' parlor.[2] Finally, the angered bishop was marched up the nave of the basilica by the two guards, whose halberds were at the level. He later charged that the whole incident had been engineered by wily Cardinal Gambatto, who supposedly wished to keep him from voting on the Schema on Holy Madness.

We must close our letter now and go to watch the fireworks display in the Circus Maximus. It is rumored that one of the displays will spell out Tertullian's maxim *Credo quia absurdum,* which was adopted as the Council's motto after it was decided that absurdity is a sufficient basis for faith.

---

[1] This bathroom in the Vatican was filled with lascivious paintings by Raphael. "Enough to have turned the lusty Aretine's liver green," said Spigonari, the seventeenth-century pornographer. The bathroom is now lost, having been either walled up or converted. Those Popes who have been asked about the bathroom's whereabouts have merely frowned.

[2] It might be said, in the guard's defense, that the present-day costume of a Rumanian prelate is a maroon business suit with wide sateen lapels. A purple tie covered with gold x's serves as pectoral cross, and the staff is optional.

X

A CHAPLET OF DEVOTIONS, CAUSES, AND SOCIETIES TO WHICH THE CATHOLIC MAY SAFELY ADHERE

One question that echoes today from the portico of St. Peter's to the pamphlet rack of St. Patrick's is: Will the advocates of this so-called "aggiornamento" denude the Church of all its special clubs and devotions? Father Tarcisius, writing in *The Vagrant,* doesn't think so:

> If these folk-singing, altar-swerving, delatinizing renegade altar boys think that they're going to gaily take a hatchet to all our fine clubs, sodalities, and leagues, they're not counting on the steel of community resistance. I am confident that the pendulum is swinging back, and our young people will soon realize that they still need a kind of spiritual rug-hooking party to keep them out of parked cars and picket lines. As for private devotions, they are secure in the knobbly hands of old parishioners who still faithfully clutch holy-card-stuffed prayer-

books and medallions rubbed smooth by contemplative fingers.

Those who agree with Father Tarcisius will be glad to see this pinfold of approved devotions and clubs, which are like rocks we can cling to in the rising tide of indifferentism masquerading as reform:

1. *The St. Contraceptua Youthful Anti-Smut League.*

This society is named for St. Contraceptua Brown of Fogarty, Iowa, who died in 1955 when a young man she knew lured her up to his apartment and then began reading to her from the works of Henry Miller. She broke out into a series of eventually fatal screaming fits, though before she died she managed to tear the books to bits and crawl into the corridor so that she might not die in a compromising situation. A young electronics addict next door was recording an opera at the time, so that today one may buy a record of the actual screams of the saint.

The Anti-Smut League's members have preserved into their young adulthood the chaste rules they learned from their grade school nuns. Consequently the girls never wear patent leather shoes, since the shiny surface reflects what the wearer has on under her dress. The men bathe in purple-colored bath water and carry carved sticks which they use to tuck their shirts into their pants. All have installed in their homes tickers which give them up-to-the-minute reports on Legion of Decency ratings. The League's moderator is Father Clodian Gumpert, author of such pamphlets as *So You Think Chastity Is a Joke!*, *Keep Your Hands to Yourself*, *The Topless Bathing Suit and the Bottomless Pit*, and *After Marriage: All Systems GO?*

2. *The Knights of the White Sepulchre.*

The members of this ancient order are often found in the vanguard of the Army of Truth, hewing mightily with the twin swords of Catholic Action and Community Reaction. In fact, the Knights are often referred to as the Church's Shock Troops (up until 1939, they liked to be called God's Panzer Division). In 1950, a contingent of these militant laymen encircled the Bozo Theatre in Strunk, Nebraska, which was at that time playing *Tumid Awakening*, a C film. For three days these embattled soldiers, protected by a rampart of overturned cars and torn-up paving stones, held off the Police and Fire Departments of Strunk, though they were persuaded in the end to leave the vigil to a cordon of nuns. Only last year, the Knights finally subjugated a druggist in Lumber Falls, Colorado, who had been selling the well-known smut magazines *Lust Panty, Groin,* and *Man's Rape.* After starvation tactics failed, the Knights sent in emetic-stuffed children, who vomited copiously on the magazine rack, thereby symbolizing the effect such trash has on tiny impressionable minds.

The White Sepulchre of Armbruster, Pennsylvania, which gives the order its name, is a plaster cast of the Holy Sepulchre in Jerusalem, and every October it is the scene of weird and picturesque rites at the society's annual convention. The Knights first don their suits of genuine steel armor and clank majestically down the town's main street, chanting *"Ha-Du-Ku-Ba-Saïd-Na,"* which means "This is surely the White Sepulchre." When the Sepulchre is reached, it inevitably turns out to be filled with beer, which spurts from apertures into the upturned helmets of the members, who drink until, one by one, they topple with a jingly crash. No one ever gets hurt at these rallies, and the reports that the Knights sometimes handcuff people to railroad tracks were probably started by the *POAU*.

3. *The Devotion to the Vestal Verger.*

Quite a large public cult has sprung up around Hamish Runcet, the now retired mystic who was from 1889 to 1925 the verger of St. Edwy's, King and Giant, in the English town of Sluicegate Weirs. Hamish never allowed the sanctuary light in St. Edwy's to go out, though he stopped using beeswax

The Knights of the White Sepulchre

candles in 1903. He explains why in his autobiography, *Exfoliations from the Blazing Tulip:*

> One day, as I was gathering a bouquet of bishop's buttons in my garden, I saw a bee violating a flower. I stood rooted to the spot with horror as the gross beast gorged its swinish gullet on the pristine pollen of the weakly screaming flower. Finally, his hoggish repast over, the bee staggered drunkenly away, humming unconcernedly, and I sank into a swound. As I lay there I heard (as it were) a voice crying "The bee is unclean. Use not his gummy secretions." From that day I stopped using beeswax candles. I tried bacon drippings and gelatin as substitutes for a while, though I now use candles made from earwax. Human earwax, that is.

The Vestal Verger was also known for his ability to read the minds of parishioners: he often stood in the vestibule of St. Edwy's at the end of Sunday Mass and told people their sins and what they had had for breakfast. But his clairvoyance mysteriously disappeared one day when an unrepentant sinner gave him a nasty crack behind the ear with the whangee handle of an umbrella. As a substitute, the Verger took up rhabdomancy, or rod divination, and to this day one may see in the sacristy of St. Edwy's the

The Vestal Verger, Hamish Runcet

iron kettles, flatirons, and broken bottles unearthed by his craft.

Perhaps the most famous incident in his life occurred when an angel finished the Verger's job of sweeping the church for him. The weary cleric had fallen asleep in the middle of his task, and when he awoke (still leaning on his broom) he found the floor swept and the dust miraculously turned to gold. The Verger's account of this incident is found in one of his letters to Clotilde, the Mad Nun of Ouvrage (see *Letters to an Astigmatic Stigmatic,* published by Gasogene Books).

Today Hamish Runcet lives in a remodeled Kentish oasthouse, and makes indulgence bags for children. Though he seldom receives visitors, the ex-Verger still issues predictions at the rate of fifty a year. On the feast of All Hallows, 1965, he predicted that:

- President Johnson will turn out to be a brass automaton with clockwork insides, operated from the planet Buggog.
- Charles de Gaulle will turn out to be the angel Abdiel, whose ambition is to reverse the direction of the earth's spin.
- In 1980 Bishop Pike will be burned at the stake in the Rose Bowl, by the order of Governor Wayne.

- A Jesuit Air Force will strafe and bomb world centers of atheism.
- The wax statue of Pius XII in St. Patrick's Cathedral will be given the power to see and hear and will some day rule New York.

Those wishing to know more about the Vestal Verger should see Puccini's opera *Il Monasterio Segreto* (*The Turkish Bedstead*), which is based on the Verger's early life.

XI

MOTHER XIMENES' HANDBOOK FOR GRADE SCHOOL NUNS

I. Things Catholic Children Should Know

1. The equator is eight thousand miles long. Do not accept contradiction on this point.

2. The uranium story: Once a little boy was digging in his back yard, and he found a piece of uranium. He held it up in the air, and a plane which was passing overhead stopped dead. It did not move on until the little boy buried the uranium again. That's how they found out what uranium can do.

3. The mother of St. Louis IX of France said to him when he was a boy: "I would rather see you fry in hell than ever see you commit a mortal sin."

4. There is a priest living in the walls of St. Sophia's Church in Constantinople. He will come out when the church is returned to Christian hands.

5. The ouiji board story: A group of irreverent young people were playing with an ouiji board one night, and they asked it if there was a God. The ouiji

board said YES and the roof fell in, killing everybody.

*II. Ways to Cultivate the Fear of Dying in Mortal
Sin*

1. Point out how difficult it is to make a *perfect*
Act of Contrition just before death. To prove it,
have your students put their heads down on their
desks and imagine that they are dying horribly, miles
from any priest. Then ask them to try to be sorry for
their sins without being afraid of Hell. If any of them
think they can do it, punish them.

2. Tell this story: Once there was an old man who
hadn't gone to Mass or Communion for years. When-
ever he got sick, he would call a priest, but every
time the priest came, the old man would say "You
can go away. I feel better now." Well, one dark,
windy night the old man became deathly ill, and he
tried to get a priest. It was midnight, so all the priests
at the church were asleep, and no one answered the
phone. Then the old man sent his little daughter to
the church to fetch a priest, and when she got there
the rectory and church were dark and still. The wind
howled cheerlessly, and there were unexplained
rustlings in the bushes. The little girl rattled the
doors and pounded on the windows, but nobody
came. Then she noticed a little window in which a

flickering red light was burning, but before she could try it a deep voice from behind the windowpane said, "Go home. There will be no priest for this man tonight." The little girl ran home and told everyone what had happened, and everyone remarked that it was strange a priest should say such a thing. Later it was discovered that the window was *in the chapel!* The old man died miserably, of course.

3. Make your students memorize the Litany for a Happy Death, which may be found on p. 1017 of the complete *Breviarum Defunctorum*. It runs thus:

> When the numbing chill of my last illness
>> creeps slowly northward from my stony toes . . .
>>> *Then God Help Me!*
>
> When my skin turns slowly from its normal
>> peachy hue to the color of cream cheese . . .
>>> (RESPONSE AS BEFORE)
>
> When my red corpuscles can hardly drag themselves along the footpaths of my arteries . . .
>>> (RESPONSE)
>
> When my pores, like tiny mouths, are gasping for life, and some of them are collapsing with an audible sigh . . .
>>> (RESPONSE)
>
> When the rattling in my throat drowns out the clatter of my beads . . .
>>> (RESPONSE)

When the dreary moaning about my bed has
   changed to an expectant hush . . .

> (RESPONSE)

When the fading breath of life dribbles fitfully
   from my chalky lips . . .

> (RESPONSE)

And when at last Sister Death comes to drag me
   away . . .

> *Deliver me to the*
> *right address!*
> Amen.

III. *Conversion Tactics*

If you have, say, a little girl in your class whose
mother is Protestant, do at least some of the following things:

1. Lecture at great length on the sorrows of a
mixed marriage.

2. Say things like "Susie, your mother isn't
Catholic, is she?" and tell her that her mother might
be converted through prayer and good example.

3. Mention to the class that Protestants have a
funny way of saying the "Our Father." Ask Susie if
this isn't so.

4. Point out that Protestants can get to Heaven
but that when they get there they may not know what
it's all about.

Study Guide for
ADVENTURES in ARITHMETIC
GRADES 3 & 4

1. Count the devils in the picture.
2. How many Evil Children are being tortured?
3. Why do the children deserve what they're getting?

Page from a Catholic Grade School Study Guide

IV. Ways of Raising Money

1. "Raffle Your Grandmother Out of Purgatory." This kind of drawing has always been successful. The winner gets a plenary indulgence for some deceased member of his family. Not that one can buy indulgences, of course; that was settled long ago. But one can make donations.

2. At Christmas have your students sell sick-call kits door-to-door. Some children persist in calling them "death kits," but this should be discouraged.

3. Have drives of all kinds: paper drives, bottle cap drives, jelly jar drives. The students who work the hardest should be given a reward. For instance, you might let them make new paper covers for the textbooks.

4. Point out to your students that the sisters will starve if thoughtful mothers do not deluge them with pies, cakes, and assorted pastries.

V. The May Procession

This event should be prepared for by months of rehearsal in the church. Though the students will be missing class time during these months, they can recite Our Father's and Hail Mary's, and you had better see to it that they do. The collected prayers can be put into a Spiritual Bouquet for the pastor. By way of encouragement, you might tell your students that the U.S. record is held by St. Semina's grade school in Los Angeles, which once amassed 9,686,723 Hail Mary's, together with a comparable number of Our Father's and Solemn Doxologies, in two months. The bouquet was sent to the parish priest in a pickup truck.

The Human Rosary is the most important part of any May Procession. Children will fight to be made part of this living chain of tributes, and boys have been known to squabble viciously for the privilege of being an Our Father. You should choose carefully those who will make up the crucifix, taking into account height as well as moral character. And it might be well to get a fat boy to be the little round medal.

One note about May Queens: It is best for the sisters to govern the choice of the girl for this part, especially if the school has lots of boys in it. Experience shows that the boys will choose some horrid little snit who has been trolloping all over the school. Girls, on the other hand, will choose some homely thing with pigeon toes and a runny nose. What you want, of course, is someone who will grow up to look like the Catholic Art Calendar representations of Mary.

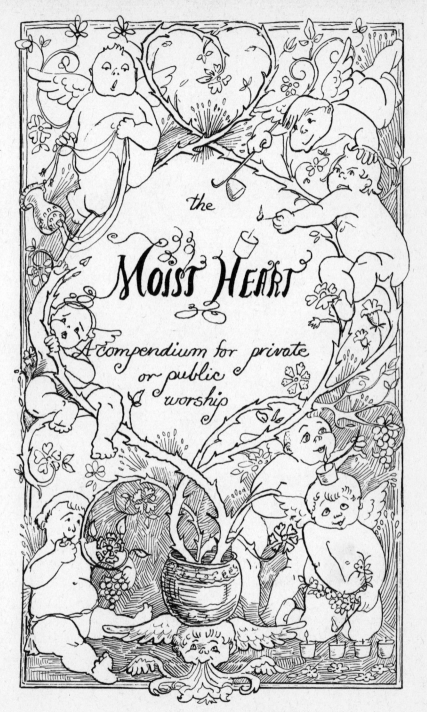

the

MOIST HEART

A compendium for private or public worship

Title page for the MOIST HEART

XII

THE MOIST HEART:
A COMPENDIUM FOR PRIVATE OR
PUBLIC WORSHIP

A May Hymn

(To the tune of "My Darling Clementine")

Mary, Mary's, not contrary,
She is fresh and pure and kind;
Round our hot and throbbing temples
We her gorgeous precepts bind.
She is Momma, she is Grandma,
And what fills us most with awe,
Logical manipulation
Can make her our Mother-in-law.

CHORUS (*to some other tune*):

        Then it's Gloriana peal the bell,
        Send the echoes down to hell,
        Make the sound all trees to fell
        With our screaming glee!

SECOND VERSE:

Plaster statues, sweetly smiling,
We will deck with fragrant weeds
While the sky's great hollow bucket
Booms the thunder of our beads!
Tear up crab grass, rip up bindweed,
Strip the wooded thickets bare,
Till an Everest of Flow'rets
Greets the unbeliever's stare.

(CHORUS)

.   .   .

Prayer for the Speedy Demise of a Bishop

(To be said by a priest whose books have been
suppressed or by an ambitious monsignor.)

O God, who dost daily sweep Thine Eternal
Dwellings, grant that the soul of the superfluous N.
may be sucked up into the Dustbag of Bliss, where
spinning motes circle ever before Thy Throne.

Prayer for Earthquakes

Oh God, Who like Samson dost jostle down pil-
lars on the heads of those who think they can do
without Thee, grant that the agnostic N. and the

secularist N. and especially the N. who passes out birth control information on street corners may find their roofs kissing their floors, with themselves in between.

Prayer for Rain
(To be chanted)

Oh God, Who dost grant the planet Venus the gift of perpetual downpour, lash our fields with blinding squalls, make deserts into steaming rain forests, and leave in the streets standing pools which testify to Your beneficence.

Prayer for Fair Weather
(Chanted more loudly, to the sound of washboards)

Oh God, Who knowest that there are some of us who live in fetid swamps which God knows do not need more rain, disregard the previous prayer, parch the mushy earth with blistering drouth, dry up the mosquito-infested dank smelly lakes of which this damned state is so proud, wither the worthless crops of those who scream for wetness, and stop the mindless everlasting pitter-patter on our leaky anodized aluminum roofs.

Commemorative Prayer for a Holy Woman
Not a Virgin

O N., who through your life didst prove that a small flaw need not lead to total corruption, turn us to the intact life which all teachers assure us is better, and teach us how we can reconcile virginity with the Church's desire for big families.

A Paradigmatic Sunday Sermon

(NOTE: *This is offered as an aid for those parish priests who don't have time to compose a new sermon for every Sunday of the year. It is a sort of sermon concentrate, which may be thinned by the skim milk of rhetoric.*)

We are all here on the launching pad of life, ready to blast off to new spiritual horizons, so let us, in this pre-countdown time, see if all the smoke that eddies from our tubes really indicates fire. You have all heard of the Mariner spacecraft that was always getting locked on the wrong star. A craft with wanderlust—a curious cruiser. The scientists, like wise fathers, had to patiently adjust the foolish machine every time it got out of line. Be sure you're properly locked in before you zoom on into the asteroid belt of temptation, where brightly tinted meteorites will clink on your hull, as if beckoning you astray.

The Paradigmatic Sunday Sermon

Always remember, while you are on the stage of this world, that God is waiting in the wings, and may unexpectedly give you the hook. God, the eternal stage-door Johnny, with flowers for the good performer and a good caning for the bad actor. Stay off the trap doors of lust! And follow the prompter, you parish priest, who gives you the best lines and fills in when you stumble or, worse, try to improvise.

A man trying to root out the rotten spots in his

life is like a soldier combing the trees with his eye in search of snipers. When you zero in on the devil of Avarice, or Lechery, or anything that moves, let him have it—whammo!—right between the eyes. Sometimes, though, in fighting entrenched evils, you have to wheel in what I call the big guns of Spirituality: Prayer, Sacrifice, and Good Counsel. Blaze away with them at the gooks, and see if it doesn't work! With different ammunition, you can use this same heavy artillery to storm the jeweled gates of Heaven and get the kind of booty that's worth a lifelong siege. And when you get near the enemy wire, don't try to cut it yourself. Let Christ run the interference. Let Him spray the corrupt foxholes with bullets from the burp gun of Sanctifying Grace. You will cross No Man's Land by treading on the willingly scattered bodies of the Saints, and you will reach GHQ with Mission Accomplished. Amen.

(Note: This kind of sermon may be extended by the use of such concepts as:

1. The candy store of indulgences.
2. The pom-pom gun of daily Communion.
3. Wearing down God's resistance by daily Mass.
4. Purgatory as a bread line.
5. Getting into Heaven by slipping under the barbed wire fence: Point out how a good confession at the End can wipe away a lifetime of brutish living, disgusting habits, and Massless Sundays.)

A typical Catholic parishoner during a sermon